Topspin

Topspin

The Story of Dr. James Bazell Stafford, Jr.

James B. Stafford, III

Gotham Books
30 N Gould St.
Ste. 20820, Sheridan, WY 82801
https://gothambooksinc.com/

© 2022 James B. Stafford III. All rights reserved.

No part of this book may be reproduced, stored in a retrieval system, or transmitted by any means without the written permission of the author.

Published by Gotham Books (January 14, 2023)

ISBN: 979-8-88775-184-9 (sc)
ISBN: 979-8-88775-185-6 (e)

Because of the dynamic nature of the Internet, any web addresses or links contained in this book may have changed since publication and may no longer be valid.

The views expressed in this work are solely those of the author and do not necessarily reflect the views of the publisher, and the publisher hereby disclaims any responsibility for them.

CONTENTS

Chapter 1 The Beginning 1

Chapter 2 College 7

Chapter 3 Military Service &
          The 335th Station Hospital 9

Chapter 4 Off to Peoria, Illinois 17

Chapter 5 Life in Peoria, Illinois 25

Chapter 6 Topspin 31

Miscellaneous Pictures 36

CHAPTER 1

The Beginning

WHEN I STARTED writing this book, I began to realize what an amazing person I had for a father. A student, an Eagle Scout, a football player, a soldier, a tennis player, a leader, and a man of God are all meaningful roles in his life that helped to shape the man he is today. I also saw him ride his motorcycle until he was eighty years old, and believe it or not he still plays tennis three to four times a week, year round, at the age of ninety-four.

I never realized how my dad truly influenced my life until I started writing this book to tell his story. I said, this is his story and not about me, that may come later, much later.

Dr. James B. Stafford, Jr, my dad, was born in Alton, Illinois, on September the 16th 1921, to James Bazell Stafford, Sr. and Mary Jane Killion Stafford. Doc Stafford's parents also gave birth to another son named Stanley, who died at birth. Mary Jane Stafford was from

**James B. Stafford, Sr. &
Mary Jane Stafford**

Carlyle, Illinois, a small town in Southern Illinois. Dad's mother met his dad in Ottumwa, Iowa, where she worked as a maid for a rich white family in Oskaloosa, Iowa, not far from Ottumwa, Iowa. His dad went to Ottumwa, Iowa, sometime before World War 1, looking for work. He found work there with John Morrell Packing House until the start of World War I (WW I) which began a short time later.

My dad's mother had two sisters, who also lived and worked in Oskaloosa as maids. Their names were Bertha Killion Campbell and Bessie Killion Russell. Mary Jane's maiden name was Mary Jane Killion. Mary Jane had two brothers who remained in Carlyle, Illinois. Their names were Otto Killion and Gus Killion. Not much is known about my dad's father's family. It is believed that he had a half-brother and some cousins. My dad was only familiar with two cousins of which he met, but my grandfather did not reveal much about his family and past. For example, my dad said that Grandpa was born in Sandusky, Ohio, but it is believed that he was really born in Louisiana around New Orleans. My dad also believed that the name Stafford was not his real name and that those who knew his real name were sworn to secrecy. All of whom have now passed away and it appears that we will never really know the origin of Stafford. We feel that my grandfather's first cousin knew the whole story. Her name was Vesta Elizabeth Williams and she lived in Shreveport, Louisiana. She died on March 18th, 2000 and Dad was never able to talk to her about my grandfather's, family. She was born January 14, 1907.

After World War I Grandfather migrated to Carlyle, Illinois; but the job possibilities were better for blacks in Alton, Illinois, so they moved there and Grandpa went to work for Western Military Academy as a chef. Now, the interesting point of this is that my grandfather had no experience as a cook but somehow he got the job. What I do know and remember and it was articulated by my dad, Grandpa was very smart, aggressive and a fast learner. These traits I believe helped him to become successful as a chef at Western Military Academy. The move to Alton took place around 1920 - 1921, however, we are not absolutely sure. The first place of residence for the Staffords was on Rock Street.

My dad was born on September 16, 1921, not long after the birth and death, of his new born baby brother Stanley. After moving to Alton the Staffords found that many of their relatives were already there.

My dad was educated in the Alton School District. The first school he attended was Dunbar Elementary School, named after Paul Laurence Dunbar. Most of the schools that blacks attended at that time were named after famous black personalities who were advocates for civil rights and equal opportunities in all areas of life. After leaving Dunbar Elementary School, he attended Elijah P. Lovejoy Jr. High, which bore the name of an abolitionist against slavery.

Because Lovejoy was so strongly against slavery, he became a very unpopular man. He printed newspaper articles that demanded the abolition of slavery. His printing press was destroyed there in Alton, Illinois, because of his stance against slavery.

At that time Lovejoy Jr. High was seventh grade to ninth grade. After completing the ninth grade, Dad went to the segregated Alton Senior High School where blacks could not participate in any extracurricular activities including athletics. All black students' lockers were on the first floor immediately as you walked into the school. The interesting point about this story is that kids could go to a segregated elementary school but later would attend an integrated high school.

My dad, who was quite an athlete and still is today, along with other black boys who played sports, could not play for the high school he attended. So they formed their own team and played other towns and schools under the name of Lovejoy Jr. High School.

While my dad was attending Dunbar Elementary, his father became president of the PTA and helped the school to gain funding for academic and athletic programs.

He kept pushing the school superintendent about funding for blacks whom he knew did not have access to the best equipment like the white students had on their playground. Grandpa also managed to build a very large and functional

PTA at Dunbar School that became recognized in the Upper Alton area as one of the best.

Grandpa was also very active in the American Legion and soon became commander of Allen Bevenue Post 354 named after two black men from Alton. Of course at this time, blacks could not become members of the VFW or American Legion, which is integrated today. He also worked with organizations that encouraged young youth from dropping out of school. At this time many black students did not finish high school. Finishing high school at this time was quite an achievement. One of the organizations that focused on this task was the Dad's Club of Salu Park. Salu Park was the park in Upper Alton where all the black kids played. In the summer the park provided various programs for the kids, because the black kids were prohibited from playing at the larger white schools. The kids from Upper Alton were very proud of their playground. Grandpa soon became president of this organization.

Later Grandpa became active in the Boy Scout program and started Troop 21 for black boys in Alton. He was the scoutmaster of Troop 21 for almost 21 years and became known as Mr. Scoutmaster. A book came out in Alton identifying outstanding blacks in the city and he was highlighted as being a great scout leader and scoutmaster. He was so notable that many black boys wanted to join Troop 21.

As a result of my grandfather's work in the Boy Scouts, he was able to become the first black to receive the coveted Silver

Beaver Award in Alton. His major goal was to help encourage black boys to stay in scouting and become Eagle Scouts. He accomplished this goal by seeing four members of his troop, including my dad to make Eagle Scout.

While writing this I realized that it was scouting that had a big influence in my father's life and how he lived it. It was the Scout Law that he used as his guiding light. For example, a scout is trustworthy, loyal, helpful, friendly, courteous, kind, obedient, cheerful, thrifty, brave, clean, and reverent. Those who were serious about scouting took each one of the laws and applied it to his life and it meant something to him in his development as a man.

CHAPTER 2

College

DAD LEFT ALTON in 1939, to attend college. He initially matriculated at Drake University in Des Moines, Iowa, where he played football. However, he did not stay at Drake long because of discrimination. In some states where the football team played, blacks could not play nor stay with the team if they stayed over night. Therefore, he decided to transfer to a university/college where he could play without having to deal with the issue of discrimination. So he transferred to Iowa Wesleyan College in Mt. Pleasant, Iowa. Iowa Wesleyan played all of its games in the state of Iowa which was more accepting of black players on local college teams.

At the time Dad attended Iowa Wesleyan, there were only three blacks on campus and they all played football. There were no girls at the time on campus. This was in the year of 1941.

The other blacks on campus along with my dad lived with the college custodian, because there were no accommodations for blacks at the college to live on campus. As you can imagine the social life was limited as well. The guys had to drive to

Burlington, Iowa, where one of the older black football players knew a family who befriended the three black students/football players and took them in as part of the family. Of course it didn't hurt that the family had three daughters who would drive to the college as guests to participate in campus social activities.

Rumblings of World War II were being heard in the background while Dad was in college, and many of his football teammates were enlisting into the military. Resonation of the war, and the treatment of the Jews by the Germans was echoing around the world. Many of the young men of the United States were interested in joining the service. My dad was dealing with the same anxiety of wanting to go off to the war. Manifested by the fact that veterans could get their education paid for by the government through the GI Bill after completion of active duty was a strong enticement to enlist to go to war. In addition his dad was also a WW I veteran and as a result that influence also lived in many of my dad's friends whose fathers's were WW I veterans. Even though there was still discrimination, the common thought was in order to make change in the United States, one must also show his commitment to the constitutional ideals of the United States. Therefore, my dad was not deterred from entering the military.

CHAPTER 3

Military Service & The 335th Station Hospital

WHILE AT IOWA Wesleyan my dad became interested in joining the military. There was much talk about joining the military and going off to fight for the United States. Many of the men who played football with Dad decided to leave school and join the military. He first went to the Navy, but he could not get past the vision requirements. He then went to the Air Force where he discovered he really wanted to be a member. He still had a problem of passing the vision test. The Air Force, and the Navy, however, had a reputation at this time of discriminating against minorities. Those circumstances led him to the Army who had a reputation of accepting everyone no matter what. So after the third attempt of trying to join the Army, he was accepted. The thought of going into Officer Candidate School to become an officer in the armed services never left his mind, and it was ever present.

As soon as he reached his basic training assignment, he went to talk to the company commander to let him know that he wanted to go to OCS (Officer Candidate School). The company commander smiled and said, "you haven't even completed basic training yet." My dad's purpose was to plant the seed that he was a leader, and that he wanted to display those leadership talents as an officer.

After being assigned to Camp Pickett, Virginia, he was assigned to a medical unit. He found out later that he would spend the majority of his military experience in a medical unit.

After spending time at Camp Pickett, he gained his wish and was sent to Camp Barkley, Texas, to Officer Candidate School (OCS). There he became a second lieutenant in the Medical Administration Corps of the US Army. After completing OCS, he was sent to Ft. Huachuca, Arizona, where he became adjutant of the 335th Station Hospital. The 335th Station Hospital was sent to Burma, to open a military hospital on the Ledo Road in Burma. The 335th Station Hospital was an all black hospital commanded by black officers and run by black enlisted men and nurses.

Let me inject this one important fact at Fort Huachuca, Dad met his future wife who was also in the military. During August of 1943, Dad met Evelyn Serena Smith who was a second

Evelyn Serena (Smith) Stafford

lieutenant in the Women's Army Auxiliary Corps, also known as a WAAC.

My mother joined the WAACs after graduating from Illinois State University with a degree in home economics. Her plan was to eventually teach the subject of home economics. Later on the name of Women's Army Auxiliary Corps (WAAC) was changed to Women's Army Corps. One day during August 1943, Mom was sitting at a table with a group of WAACS and several other black officers in the Officer's Club. Dad and a group of his officer friends walked in and saw these ladies sitting at the table and they walked over to them. My dad said to the other officers sitting at the table that the women they were sitting with were already spoken for, and that they belonged to them. That was the beginning of the romance between my dad and mom. They only dated three months after that encounter and decided to get married in December of 1943. One could say that Dad swept my mom off of her feet.

Mom and Dad Lieutenants

Mom was born and reared in Muskogee, Oklahoma. Her family had earlier moved to California. Mom's older sister, Kathryn Smith who later married Clement Maynard attended Illinois State University as well. Mom, you might say, followed her sister there.

Mom and Dad married in St. Louis, Missouri, at Aunt Emm's house. They were married by Dad's hometown minister, the Rev. Little, pastor of Union Baptist Church in Alton, Illinois. They didn't have much of an opportunity to stay together because Dad received orders to ship out to Burma as a member of the 335th Station Hospital, and Mom had to return to her initial duty station at Ft. Des Moines, Iowa.

Mom had to resign her commission in the military because she was pregnant with my sister who was born in Torrence, California, on April 9, 1945. At this time a woman could not be pregnant and remain in the military, so mom left the Army and moved to California to live with her mother. I came into the world two years later in Chicago, Illinois.

It was amazing to know that during my dad's time at OCS while he was being trained as an officer with white officer candidates there were no problems at all. When they graduated, the black and white officers took different paths. At that time black officers could not command white troops; so the officers that graduated with my dad were assigned to all black units.

The 335th Station Hospital was to be an all black hospital. My dad and two other officers were the first complement of men to staff this hospital. After a short time a black commanding officer was named to run the hospital along with all black medical officers and enlisted men. All of which had the technical skills to function in a viable hospital, regardless of the patient's race. This group of men could be similarly compared to the Tuskegee Airmen for this was the first all black hospital, staffed and operated by black officers and enlisted men and black nurses that were assigned to the hospital and flown over later to Burma.

In 1943, the 335th Station Hospital, which was a 150 bed hospital, was sent to Burma where it was set up at the 80 mile mark on what was called the Ledo Road. This all black hospital was set up with all necessary equipment to perform complete medical services to any one who needed it. The Ledo Road was built in part by all black engineers using, ironically heavy equipment such as Caterpillar manufactured equipment; yet, when these same GI's returned home to the USA, many could not find good jobs due to discrimination.

The hospital operated in Burma for approximately two years. The Ledo Road, where they were located, was built so that the Chinese could drive convoys with supplies to support their forces. At that time China and Japan were combatants. The war was over in 1945 and the hospital was preparing to leave Burma. My dad left behind many memories of what took place there and often wondered what he would find if he went back.

After serving four years in the Army serving his country it was finally time to come home. My dad left Burma on October 7, 1945, and arrived in New York on October 22, 1945. When the ship pulled into the New York harbor, my dad saw many people standing on the pier waving and saying "Welcome Home." Tears welled in my dad's eyes as he looked in jubilation, realizing that probably nothing had changed regarding blacks gaining equality in America. He later found just how right he was. As a result he vowed to do all that he could to work toward changing living conditions for blacks here in the United States. He carries this vow with him today. At ninety-four years of age my dad and my mother too are still working toward equality for blacks in America.

After being discharged from the Army my dad went back to his hometown of Alton, Illinois. He contacted his wife and daughter who were still in Los Angeles, California, to go to Alton. Before my dad entered the military, he wanted to be an optometrist. He later entered Monroe College of Optometry in Chicago, Illinois, (now called Illinois College of Optometry). He graduated in 1947 shortly after my birth. My dad opened his practice in Alton, Illinois, for only a short period of time.

Even though he was discharged from active duty, he still remained in the reserves. As a result, he was called back into active duty for the Korean Conflict. However, this time he was called back as an optometrist in the Medical Services Corps. After being called back, Dad spent some time at Fort

Riley, Kansas, and Fort Dix, New Jersey. His family also went with him to both locations.

He later received orders to go to the Ryukyus Army Hospital on Okinawa as an optometrist.

Dad's second tour of duty was quite different from the first; President Truman had issued orders stating that there would be no more segregation in the armed services. Unlike his tour of duty at the 335th Station Hospital on Ledo Road in Burma, Dad now examined all patients regardless of their race, creed, or color.

Mom, Dad, Sylvia and Me

My dad was in Okinawa for about six months in 1952 before he requested to have his family join him. The military provided us with housing and with a school to attend. I was five years old and my sister Sylvia was seven. We both attended school while in Okinawa. Sylvia and I

Our home in Okinawa

had a fun time going to school and living in Okinawa. Living and going to school in Okinawa are once in a life time experiences that my sister and I will never forget. We lived in a small white house with shudders as part of the officers' quarters. It made us feel as if we were somebody. My sister and I really didn't know just how isolated we were from what was really going on in the world but especially in the United States where blacks still couldn't drink from the same water fountain in some states. During this time my dad was the only black officer in the hospital on the island.

Not long after we arrived on the island, there was a government order that personnel would be reduced and even some personnel, officers and enlisted men, could be reduced in rank. As a result my dad decided to give up his commission and return to the states. He, nonetheless, did not know where he wanted to settle to raise his family and to start his optometry practice. For a while he set up his practice in Los Angeles, California, where his wife's mother and sister were currently living. However, it didn't work out for him the way he expected. Therefore, he gave thought and consideration to moving to Illinois to start his new life and to start his own practice. His wife was familiar with Illinois because she went to school there at Illinois State University and she had friends in the area. Dad also was familiar with Illinois because he grew up in Alton, Illinois.

CHAPTER 4

Off to Peoria, Illinois

WHEN DAD LEFT Okinawa and was discharged from the Army, we ended up in Los Angeles, California. This location was not foreign to us because Mom's mother and sister were making their home in Los Angeles at the time. Initially Dad thought it might be good to stay in Los Angeles and try to make a go of it there by starting his optometric practice. He, ironically had a friend there that he met at Ft. Dix, New Jersey. His name was Dr. Harold Anderson an ear, nose, and throat doctor. They got together and decided to try to set up a practice together. However, my dad found out later that the laws in California did not allow him to practice optometry there without a California license. At the time my dad was only licensed in Illinois. Nonetheless, they still tried to make a go of it. Not long after their start, they realized that it was not going to work so they decided to split.

So Dad, after approximately three years at Iowa Wesleyan College and an optometry degree from Monroe College of Optometry, found a job working for a chemical company called Post, Paint & Chemical Company.

During this time Mom was working at the Los Angeles YWCA, and they also bought a house on Wilton Place.

The Staffords continued this practice for approximately a year. Dad, however, was growing more disenchanted with this arrangement, so Mom and Dad had to decide on making a life changing decision. Dad felt as if his career was built around optometry since that was what he spent so many years trying to become. He was already licensed to practice in Illinois. Of course he could obtain a license to practice in California, but he would have to go back to school and take some additional courses. He did try that for a few months, but later felt it would take too long to complete the course of study to get licensed in California. As a result they decided to leave California and head to Illinois.

It was in the year of 1957 when we left California. Dad knew at the time that he did not want to set his practice up in his hometown of Alton, Illinois. Mom had a friend in Peoria, Illinois who told her that there was no black optometrist in Peoria, Illinois. Mom and Dad felt that Peoria was a great place because of its close proximity to Alton, Dad's home, and Chicago where many of his optometry classmates practiced.

When we moved to Peoria, we did not know anyone, because we had never been there. We really did not know what to expect. However, what we found was a city that was racially segregated. There were few if any black teachers, at the time, in the Peoria District 150 School System and only one black professor at Bradley University. Black businessmen or professionals were not allowed to set up an office or practice in the downtown area. My mom who had a degree from Illinois State University in Normal, Illinois, could not get a teaching job in Peoria at the high school but was offered one at the grade school. After looking for several months, she finally found a job working for the Department of Public Welfare as a caseworker.

One of the first individuals Dad met was a dentist named Dr. George P. Smith. Dr. Smith was very instrumental in helping Dad learn the lay of the land in Peoria. He also recommended to him the best place to set up practice. As I have already mentioned black professionals could not set up a business or practice in downtown Peoria.

1320 SW Adams St.

Finding office space in Peoria was difficult due to discrimination. Most professionals were on the outskirts of downtown, up on North Adams or in black areas of town.

Eventually, Dad found office space at 1320 SW Adams Street, not far from downtown. This location also had living space downstairs and upstairs. Our landlord was a man by the name of Max Lipkin, a businessman, who owned a small sundry store in the downtown area. My sister and I would love to go with Dad to pay the rent because he would always allow us to select candy from Mr. Lipkin's store. Dad, however, didn't like for us to take candy from his store, so eventually he would not let us go with him. My dad is a proud man and didn't want to take anything from anybody. Lipkin's son was also the city attorney for Peoria, Illinois.

We lived on Adams from the time we were in elementary school to high school, approximately nine years.

MT. ZION BAPTIST CHURCH

Now that we had a home and Dad had office space, the next step was to find a church home. After going around the city visiting different churches, we decided on Mt. Zion Baptist Church. It was located on the corner of Fourth Street and Sheridan Rd. Mt. Zion Church was pastored by Rev. M.D. Dixon and first lady Katie P. Dixon. They were very friendly to the family and really made us feel at home. So Mt. Zion Baptist Church would become our church home. As a matter of fact Mom and Dad still attend there today and are probably the oldest living members in the church today. From the onset Mom and Dad became very active in the church's activities. Mom worked in the Sunday School and Dad in the Baptist Training Union known at the time as BTU. Dad has always been an active person, not only in the church but also in the community as well.

During Dad's early years at Mt. Zion Baptist Church, the Creve Coeur Council tried to start new Boy Scout troops in the churches throughout Peoria. To my knowledge there was only one other black Boy Scout troop in Peoria and it was based at Zion Baptist Church on Seventh Street. The council asked Rev. Dixon if Mt. Zion would be interested in starting a troop. Rev. Dixon agreed and asked my dad to be the scoutmaster. Dad spent many years as a Boy Scout growing up in Alton, Illinois. His father was the scoutmaster of Troop 21 of the Piasa Council in Alton, Illinois. Dad was also one of four black boys to become the first black Eagle Scouts in the Piasa Council and his dad was their mentor and scoutmaster. It was not easy then for black boys to obtain the rank of Eagle Scout and it is still not easy today. As a matter of fact when I was in scouting at Mt. Zion, Troop 19, I only obtained the rank of first class scout.

Dad was assisted in starting Troop 19 by Gene Irving, Kermit Burton, David Duncan, and John Gwynn. The troop started out with about eight boys but grew to become more than twenty. In the beginning of Troop 19 most of the boys lived in the southern part of Peoria; however, before too long boys came from all over to join Troop 19, many from the north end. To my knowledge, one of the first black Eagle Scouts in Peoria came out of Troop 19 when my dad was the scoutmaster. His name was Milton Shaw. Some of the early members of Troop 19 were James Davis, Kenny Sydnor,

Melvin Irving, David Duncan, Mose Duncan, George Duncan, Chris Duncan, James Bryson, Patrick Leatherwood, Hal Slaughter, Eric Turner, Fred Lewis, and I. You know that when you start naming people you will leave someone out. If I have I apologize.

Dad exposed us to all things about scouting: attending camporees, scout camps, and many other scouting activities most of which were tied to obtaining one of the many scouting merit badges. Many of us would also spend a week in the summer at Camp Wokanda the Boy Scout camp near Peoria. I will never forget my experiences there. Believe it or not, at the time we were there in the early sixties, this camp had several prejudiced people attending the camp. From time to time we would come close to having physical altercations. Yeah, even Boy Scouts can be prejudiced towards blacks. The members of Troop 19, thanks to Dad, broke a lot of color barriers and we were exposed to a variety of experiences.

It goes without saying that most of the young men of Troop 19, while my dad was scoutmaster, became good citizens and successful young men. Many enrolled in college, joined the military, and obtained well paying jobs. However, no matter what they did, they all were good citizens.

Scouting introduced my dad to many different experiences. As a result I was introduced to them as well. One summer my dad was offered an opportunity to attend the Philmont Scout Ranch located in Cimarron, New Mexico. We as a family spent one week there learning about the scouting experience and how new and different scouting programs could be applied to our troop in Peoria. It was a great experience for everyone. When we were there during the early sixties, I believe, we were the only black family in attendance at the camp. My mom and dad taught both my sister and me how to get along with everyone. They knew if we were to grow intellectually and spiritually to become well rounded individuals, learning to adjust to different social environments was a necessary survival skill. He knew that throughout our lives there would be many instances where we will be the only black individuals present.

CHAPTER 5

Life in Peoria, Illinois

PEORIA, ILLINOIS, was similar to Alton, Illinois, where Dad grew up, in as much as there was segregation and discrimination. Blacks were working at Caterpillar and a few other plants, but they were not the high valued jobs. Many eating-places were not open to blacks.

The NAACP (National Association for the Advancement of Colored People) and the Commission on Human Relations were working hard to rectify some of the discrimination problems in Peoria. However, the local citizens, in general, were slow to respond. Dad became active in both the NAACP and the Commission on Human Relations. The commission was an interracial group of volunteers and Dad subsequently became secretary for the group.

Harry Sephus was president of the NAACP during the late fifties and early sixties. Dad worked with the NAACP president as they tried to improve the living conditions and job opportunities for blacks in Peoria.

There were several housing issues they were dealing with at this time, especially with the housing authority. Certain sections of Warner Homes were for blacks, and other areas of the Warner Homes were for whites. I know this issue well for from 1959 to 1962 I delivered papers in Warner Homes and I never understood why all the whites lived in one section of the projects and blacks lived in the other section. I noticed then but could not explain why the upkeep of the projects looked better in the white section than in the black.

The Taft Homes were set up for blacks and the Harrison Homes were for all whites. Mr. Fred Jolly was manager at that time and found every excuse why the many housing projects could not be integrated.

Mr. John Gwynn followed Harry Sephus as president of the NAACP. He was very instrumental in influencing racial change in Peoria. He organized many demonstrations and sit ins in Peoria. As a result hiring practices improved at CILCO and department store eating counters were opened to blacks. John Gwynn was very aggressive when it came to civil rights in Peoria. I participated on several of the NAACP demonstrations. My sister, Sylvia, was the first black individual to work at Sears downtown as a sales clerk. I later followed her when she left to go to work for Szold's Department store on the south-end.

Dad was on the education committee for the NAACP along with Mrs. Vera Irving. They spent many hours at the school board trying to convince the superintendent, at the time, to hire more black teachers. However, they were unsuccessful in this regard.

During my enrollment in the Peoria Public Schools District 150, from 1954 through 1965, when I graduated from Manual High School, I never experienced a black teacher.

In the late sixties Dad along with Richard Penelton was invited to join the Downtown Kiwanis. This was just another one of my dad's first.

Dad was a trailblazer and opened the door for other blacks in Peoria, and most people in the black community in particular did not realize it. Dad never sought recognition for himself; he just wanted a better living environment that was fair and equal for all regardless of race, creed or color.

Even though it is not well known today but on April 10, 1959, Dr. James B. Stafford became the first Negro, as we were referred to then, to hold a seat on the Peoria City Council.

Dad won the appointment by a 5 to 2 vote after they deadlocked on six previous ballots. He was to fill the seat of William W. Kumpf, who resigned to become the county recorder. My dad's name was placed into nomination by then Mayor Eugene Leiter. Those individuals who

Picture taken by the Peoria Journal Star April 1959

supported his nomination and voted for him were the mayor, and councilmen William H. Kennedy, Robert J. Lehnhausen, Ray A. Neumann, and Frederic R. Oakley. My dad hoped that his appointment would help promote better human relations in the city of Peoria. For a black man to be appointed to the city council during this time was quite an accomplishment. It was such a big deal that Jet Magazine mentioned the event in their April 30 and May 7, 1959, weekly magazine. Dad ran for re-election twice during the 1960's but his attempt failed. Peoria is a heavily Republican town and he ran as a Democrat. That was problem number one. Problem number two was the fact that he was black and the black vote did not turnout.

Illinois Valley Optometric Society

After getting his optometric practice started and we started settling down in Peoria, Dad found that some of his classmates from optometry school were members of the Illinois Valley Optometric Society. The focus of the society was to discuss and to take care of issues impacting the optometry profession. As he spent more time with this organization, he held many offices and eventually became president. While functioning as a member of the society, he also became a member of the State of Illinois Optometric Association. There he held the office of membership chairman and held this office for sometime. Based upon his participation and leadership in the organization, many members suggested that he run for state president of the Illinois Optometric Association. After long and hard work by him and members of the local association, who pledged to support his candidacy for president, they were also able to convince other societies in upstate Illinois to support him as well. He knew when he decided to run for president of the Illinois Optometric Association that there would be plenty of competition especially from upstate Illinois, and he was right for the first time he ran for this position; he was defeated. It took two tries. He was elected on the third attempt and became the first African-American to serve as president of the Illinois Optometric Association. He held this position for two years.

CHAPTER 6

Topspin

I HAVE BEEN ASKED on several occasions when did my dad start playing tennis. My answer always has been for as long as I can remember. My dad has played tennis all of my life, and he is still playing today at the age of 94. Now, I always thought I was a pretty good athlete but tennis was one sport at which I could never beat my dad.

He says that he always has been involved in athletics, played fullback on the Iowa Wesleyan University football team, played baseball and lettered in both. I couldn't out run him until I was in high school.

He was first introduced to tennis when his father, who was a chef at Western Military Academy in Alton, Illinois, was working as a chef at the YWCA girls' camp. Dad got to know a few of the female participants at the camp who showed him how to play tennis. Dad was probably still in grade school then.

In high school he participated in league play and as a result played in his first tournament. He won! He's been playing ever since. He loved this sport and still does. As a kid I remember asking him why he plays so much tennis. He said he loved playing it and it was good exercise. He tried to get my sister and me to play while we were still in junior high school. We did start taking lessons at Procter Center. However, I was more interested in playing football and basketball so I stopped and so did my sister.

As I have already mentioned, Dad has always played tennis. He even played in Burma when he was assigned to the 335th Station Hospital, the all black hospital.

While in Burma, the guys that he played tennis had to build their own tennis court in the dirt. It was still hard to get in a lot of playing time due to the frequent monsoons that would wash out the courts.

When he was still in his eighty's actually around 86, Dad played with 12 other players as a group at Glen Oak Park every Monday, Wednesday, and Friday, and he plays with five other friends at Peoria Racquet Club once a week.

Today at 94, he has cut his playing back to three times a week. However, in January 2016, he had to lay off playing tennis due to some leg and knee pain.

My dad's love for tennis is why I named his story *TOPSPIN*. Not to mention whenever I played him he would put a lot of topspin on the tennis ball. He was left-handed and he just hit a lot of topspin naturally, especially on his lob shot. This of course made the ball hard to return. It was a dangerous shot he had in his bag of tricks. I don't know today if he still hits a lot of topspin. Now in 2016, I don't play tennis at all and he is 94 going on 95 in September of 2016, and still is playing tennis…wow what a blessing that is!

Dad had many friends and acquaintances that he played tennis with. But his main tennis buddy was John Timmes, who retired from the Peoria Police Department and who is now deceased. As a matter of fact many of his tennis buddies have passed on. So now most of his tennis playing friends are younger than he is. John Timmes and David Graham both partnered with my dad to play in many doubles tournaments in Peoria and other places and won many of them.

My dad is an unusual person and in many ways non traditional. He has some of the most unusual hobbies. For many years he worked with leather. He made all kinds of different leather projects from purses to belts and saddlebags for his motorcycle. Yes, I said motorcycle. He owned and rode a motorcycle until he was approximately eighty years old. He probably still would be riding one if he had not decided to sell it, so he could buy a bi-turbo Maserati from my sister Sylvia. Well, that transaction was never consummated, so he no longer owns a motorcycle. My mother was so happy that he no longer owned and rode a motorcycle.

He also had a hobby of working with stained glass and building stained glass windows and other stained glass objects. There are still several of his projects in his home in Peoria and in his church. He donated several stained glass projects to Mt. Zion Baptist Church, his home church.

Dad on his motorcycle

For many years he was a semi-professional photographer. This is going back to the days of film and not digital. He owned several different cameras and developed his own film. My sister, Sylvia, picked up taking pictures as a hobby and also started developing her own pictures. I did a little of that as well. However, in today's time, who develops pictures. That is a lost trade now that everything is digital and everyone can now own a camera.

His work in the church is unprecedented. He is a deacon, a former treasurer and chairman of the finance committee.

In June 1995, Dad started working with Lynn Williams, Shelly Gore, Paul Slaughter, and Geraldine Henning in getting approval from United Way to open the Food Pantry at Mt. Zion Baptist Church. He has continued working with the Food Pantry up to the present time.

In 2005 Dad initiated the formation of the Westwood Neighborhood Association. Even though he was the main influence behind its establishment he never became the first association president.

I have finally come to the conclusion that I am just like my dad. How could I not be. I saw him go through these times struggling in his business but also working hard in the church. I used to watch him as he would take on various tasks such as building his office, fixing the plumbing in the house, repairing the car, and many other projects. He was a "jack of all trades." I find myself as being the same way. My wife often says that I am just like my dad. How could I have had a better role model. Dr. James Bazell Stafford, Jr, my dad, is like the TOPSPIN of the proverbial tennis ball still spinning towards his life's purpose of achievement.

Miscellaneous Pictures

Mayor of Peoria, Ill, Jim Ardis, Mom and Dad

Lieutenants James B. and Evelyn Stafford

Lieutenant Evelyn S. Stafford

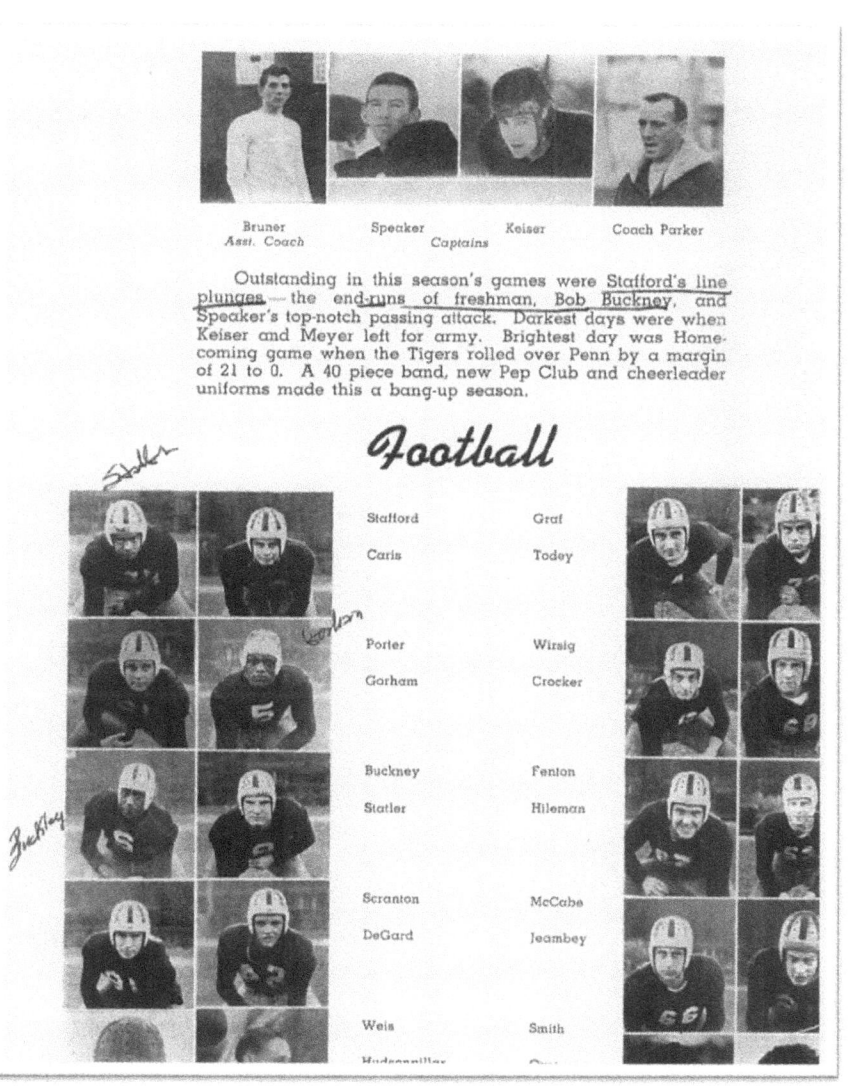

Bruner — Asst. Coach
Speaker, Keiser — Captains
Coach Parker

Outstanding in this season's games were Stafford's line plunges — the end-runs of freshman, Bob Buckney, and Speaker's top-notch passing attack. Darkest days were when Keiser and Meyer left for army. Brightest day was Homecoming game when the Tigers rolled over Penn by a margin of 21 to 0. A 40 piece band, new Pep Club and cheerleader uniforms made this a bang-up season.

Football

Stafford
Caris
Porter
Gorham
Buckney
Statler
Scranton
DeGard
Weis
Hudsonpillar

Graf
Todey
Wirsig
Crocker
Fenton
Hileman
McCabe
Jeambey
Smith

Page taken from the Iowa Wesleyan College 1942 year book

IOWA WESLEYAN COLLEGE

W

This is to Certify that

James Stafford

upon recommendation of the Director of Athletics
and by the approval of the Athletic Committee
has been awarded the

Wesleyan Varsity **W** in Football

for the season of 1941.

Eldon Parker
DIRECTOR OF ATHLETICS

CHAIRMAN OF COMMITTEE

IOWA WESLEYAN COLLEGE

W

This is to Certify that

James Stafford

upon recommendation of the Director of Athletics
and by the approval of the Athletic Committee
has been awarded the

Wesleyan Varsity **W** in Baseball

for the season of 1942.

Eldon Parker
DIRECTOR OF ATHLETICS

CHAIRMAN OF COMMITTEE

Picture(s) of Dr. Stafford on page 31, 39 and 40 were provided by Peoria Park District

Officers of the 335th Station Hospital in Burma

Lieutenant Stafford in Burma

www.ingramcontent.com/pod-product-compliance
Lightning Source LLC
LaVergne TN
LVHW061604070526
838199LV00077B/7172